I Do the Right Thing!

What Is Right?

Dwayne Booker

SOCIAL AND EMOTIONAL LEARNING FOR THE REAL WORLD™

Rosen Classroom™

I always try to do the right thing.

I help at home.
I help at school.

I talk and listen.
I'm kind to others.

I care for Earth and animals.

I learn and grow each day.
I think about what's right.

I do my part to make things better.

Words to Know

home

talk